Can you find anything else that has the same beginning sound as <u>Alvin</u>?

Apples!

Please note that for vowels *a, e, i, o,* and *u* the book only includes words and objects that start with the short vowel sound. This helps avoid confusion and emphasizes the vowel sound in words that your child will first begin to read. If you think your child is ready, you may want to explain that the vowels can also sometimes make the same sound as the letter name.

After you have gone through the book once, it may be fun and helpful to go through it again with your child. Remember to praise your child's efforts and keep the interaction fun. Try to keep these tips in mind, but don't worry about doing everything right. Simply sharing the book together will help prepare your child for reading and a lifetime of reading enjoyment!

# Can You Find?

## An ABC Book

---

*Dedicated to Sarah Poindexter*
*with special thanks for her humor and joy over many years*
*teaching children about the letters of the alphabet*

Text Copyright © 2016 by Sindy McKay
Illustrations Copyright © 2016 by Matt Loveridge
Reading Consultant: Bruce Johnson, M.Ed.

We Both Read® is a trademark of Treasure Bay, Inc.

Published by
Treasure Bay, Inc.
P.O. Box 119
Novato, CA 94948 USA

Printed in Malaysia

Library of Congress Catalog Card Number: 2015940397

Hardcover ISBN: 978-1-60115-279-4
Paperback ISBN: 978-1-60115-280-0

Visit us online at: www.TreasureBayBooks.com

PR 11-15

# Can You Find?
## An ABC Book

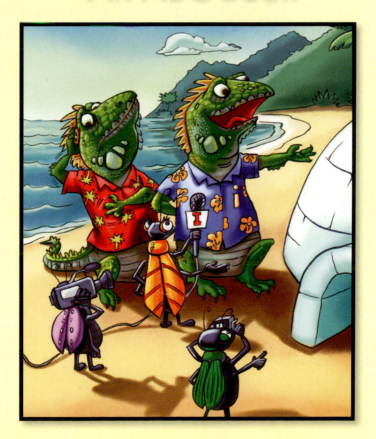

By Sindy McKay

Illustrated by Matt Loveridge

TREASURE BAY

# <u>A</u>lvin <u>a</u>dmires <u>a</u>cting.

Can you find some things in this picture that have the same beginning sound as **<u>A</u>lvin**?

These words all start with the letter **A**.
The letter **A** can be written two ways:

# A a

Can you find these letters hidden in the picture?

# **B**onnie **b**ursts **b**ubbles.

Can you find some things in this picture that have the same beginning sound as **B**onnie?

These words all start with the letter **B**.
The letter **B** can be written two ways:

# B b

Can you find these letters hidden in the picture?

# **C**onnor **c**atches **c**ows.

Can you find some things in this picture that have the same beginning sound as **Connor**?

These words all start with the letter **C**.
The letter **C** can be written two ways:

# C c

Can you find these letters hidden in the picture?

# **D**avid **d**irects **d**ucks.

Can you find some things in this picture that
have the same beginning sound as **David**?

s **e**ggs.

...at have the same

...se words all start with

...e written two ways:

...dden in the picture?

...?

## **E**llen **e**ducate

Can you find some things th
beginning sound as **Ellen**? The
the letter **E**. The letter **E** can b

# E e

Can you find these letters hi

# <u>E</u>llen <u>e</u>ducates <u>e</u>ggs.

Can you find some things that have the same beginning sound as **<u>Ellen</u>**? These words all start with the letter **E**. The letter **E** can be written two ways:

# E e

Can you find these letters hidden in the picture?

These words all start with the letter **D**.
The letter **D** can be written two ways:

# D d

Can you find these letters hidden in the picture?

# <u>F</u>rank <u>f</u>umbles <u>f</u>ruit.

Can you find some things that have the same beginning sound as **Frank**? These words all start with the letter **F**. The letter **F** can be written two ways:

# F f

Can you find these letters hidden in the picture?

# **G**lenn **g**uards **g**eckos.

Can you find some things in this picture that start with the same beginning sound as **G**lenn?

These words all start with the letter **G**.
The letter **G** can be written two ways:

# G g

Can you find these letters hidden in the picture?

# <u>H</u>ank <u>h</u>andles <u>h</u>amburgers.

Can you find some things in this picture that have the same beginning sound as **<u>H</u>ank**?

These words all start with the letter **H**.
The letter **H** can be written two ways:

# H h

Can you find these letters hidden in the picture?

# Ingrid interviews iguanas.

Can you find some things that have the same beginning sound as **Ingrid**? These words all start with the letter **I**. The letter **I** can be written two ways:

# I i

Can you find these letters hidden in the picture?

# <u>J</u>ack <u>j</u>umps over <u>j</u>elly <u>j</u>ars.

Can you find some things that start with the same
beginning sound as **<u>J</u>ack**? These words all start with
the letter **J**. The letter **J** can be written two ways:

# J j

Can you find these letters hidden in the picture?

# **K**aren **k**isses **k**oalas.

Can you find some things in this picture that start with the same beginning sound as **Karen**?

These words all start with the letter **K**.
The letter **K** can be written two ways:

# K k

Can you find these letters hidden in the picture?

# <u>L</u>aura <u>l</u>icks <u>l</u>emons.

Can you find some things in this picture that start with the same beginning sound as **<u>L</u>aura**?

These words all start with the letter **L**.
The letter **L** can be written two ways:

# L l

Can you find these letters hidden in the picture?

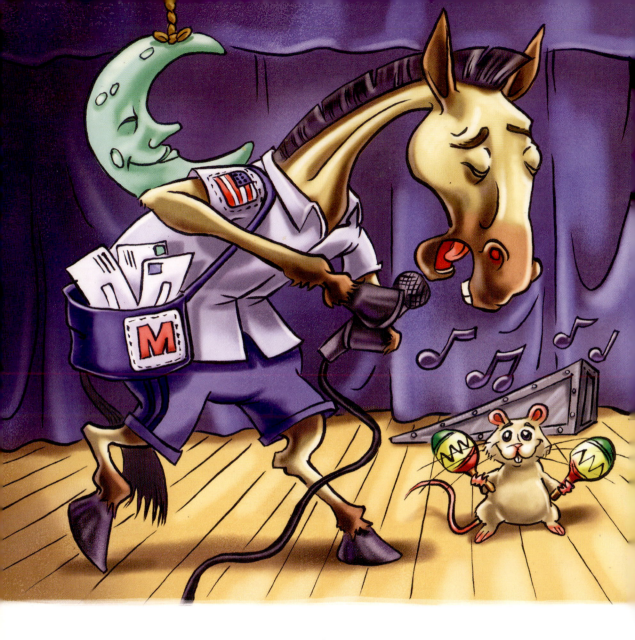

# **M**ikey **m**akes **m**usic.

Can you find some things in this picture that start with the same beginning sound as **Mikey**?

These words all start with the letter **M**.
The letter **M** can be written two ways:

# M m

Can you find these letters hidden in the picture?

# <u>N</u>ancy <u>n</u>eeds <u>n</u>apkins.

Can you find some things that have the same
beginning sound as **<u>N</u>ancy**? These words all start with
the letter **N**. The letter **N** can be written two ways:

# N n

Can you find these letters hidden in the picture?

# <u>O</u>scar <u>o</u>perates <u>o</u>ften.

Can you find some things that start with the same beginning sound as **<u>Oscar</u>**? These words all start with the letter **O**. The letter **O** can be written two ways:

Can you find these letters hidden in the picture?

# **P**aul **p**roudly **p**lays **p**iano.

Can you find some things in this picture that start with the same beginning sound as **Paul**?

These words all start with the letter **P**.
The letter **P** can be written two ways:

# P p

Can you find these letters hidden in the picture?

# **Q**uincy **q**uacks **q**uietly.

Can you find some things that have the same
beginning sound as **Quincy**? These words all start with
the letter **Q**. The letter **Q** can be written two ways:

# Q q

Can you find these letters hidden in the picture?

# <u>R</u>obin <u>r</u>ecognizes <u>r</u>ain.

Can you find some things that start with the same beginning sound as **Robin**? These words all start with the letter **R**. The letter **R** can be written two ways:

# R r

Can you find these letters hidden in the picture?

# **S**arah **s**leeps **s**oundly.

Can you find some things in this picture that start with the same beginning sound as **S**arah?

These words all start with the letter **S**.
The letter **S** can be written two ways:

# S s

Can you find these letters hidden in the picture?

# <u>T</u>om <u>t</u>aps <u>t</u>errifically.

Can you find some things in this picture that start with the same beginning sound as **<u>T</u>om**?

These words all start with the letter **T**.
The letter **T** can be written two ways:

# T t

Can you find these letters hidden in the picture?

# <u>U</u>ncle <u>U</u>nger <u>u</u>nloads <u>u</u>mbrellas.

Can you find some things that have the same beginning sound as **<u>Uncle</u>**? These words all start with the letter **U**. The letter **U** can be written two ways:

# U u

Can you find these letters hidden in the picture?

# <u>V</u>ictor <u>v</u>acuums <u>v</u>igorously!

Can you find some things that start with the same beginning sound as **<u>V</u>ictor**? These words all start with the letter **V**. The letter **V** can be written two ways:

# V v

Can you find these letters hidden in the picture?

# <u>W</u>alter <u>w</u>ashes <u>w</u>hales.

Can you find some things in this picture that have the same beginning sound as **<u>W</u>alter**?

These words all start with the letter **W**.
The letter **W** can be written two ways:

# W w

Can you find these letters hidden in the picture?

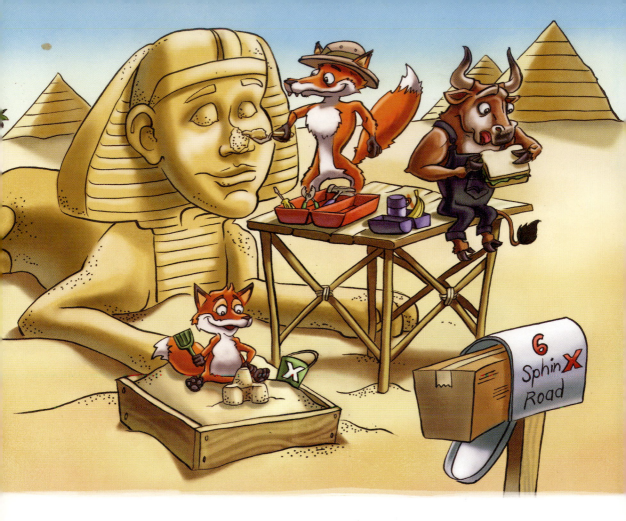

# Re<u>x</u> can fi<u>x</u> a Sphin<u>x</u>.

Can you find some things in this picture that _end_
with the same sound as **Re<u>x</u>**? These words _end_ with
the letter **X**. The letter **X** can be written two ways:

# X x

Can you find these letters hidden in the picture?

# <u>Y</u>ani <u>y</u>elped <u>y</u>esterday.

Can you find some things that have the same beginning sound as **<u>Y</u>ani**? These words all start with the letter **Y**. The letter **Y** can be written two ways:

# Y y

Can you find these letters hidden in the picture?

# **Z**elda **z**oomed **z**estfully.

Can you find some things that have the same beginning sound as **Z**elda? These words all start with the letter **Z**. The letter **Z** can be written two ways:

# **Z z**

Can you find these letters hidden in the picture?

# The Alphabet

Aa   Bb   Cc   Dd

Ee   Ff   Gg   Hh

Ii   Jj   Kk   Ll

Mm   Nn   Oo   Pp

Qq   Rr   Ss   Tt

Uu   Vv   Ww   Xx

Yy   Zz

If you liked **Can You Find?**, here is another
We Both Read® book you are sure to enjoy!

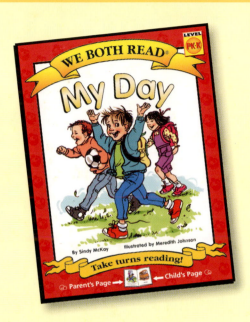

## My Day

This book is designed for the child who is just being introduced to reading. The child's pages have only one or two words, which relate directly to the illustration and even rhyme with what has just been read to them. This title is a charming story about what a child does in the course of a simple happy day.